101
things to see
in Cornwall

Robert Hesketh

Bossiney Books • Exeter

First published 2021 by
Bossiney Books Ltd, 68 Thorndale Courts, Whitycombe Way,
Exeter, EX4 2NY
www.bossineybooks.com

ISBN 978-1-906474-90-4
Acknowledgements
The maps are by Graham Hallowell
All photographs are by the author, www.roberthesketh.co.uk
or from the publisher's own collection

Printed in Great Britain by Booths Print, Penryn

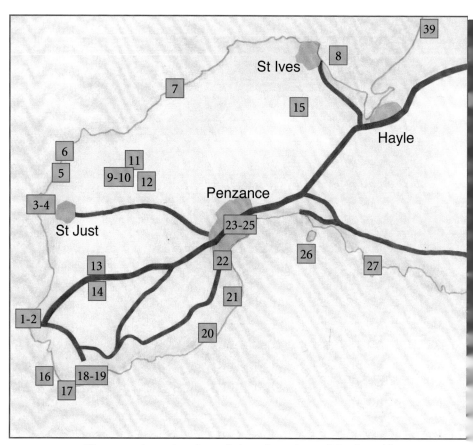

The approximate locations of places in and near West Penwith

What's included?

We decided to exclude anywhere with an admission charge, which meant omitting some fantastic places, from the Eden Project to Cotehele House and Geevor Mine, though some places such as Levant Mine have much to be seen from the outside.

We hope the selection will help you enjoy your holiday to the full without great expense.

The information given was accurate at the time of going to press, but parking and entry charges are subject to change.

1 Land's End

England's most westerly point is justly famed for its spectacular scenery. The Land's End Experience year-round theme park offers a varied programme of events, refreshment areas, souvenir shops, visitor centre, toilets, accommodation and the RSPB Discovery Centre. Entry is free, but parking, the interactive cinema, interactive animations and children's farm are ticketed.

2 Sennen Cove

Sennen Cove has one of Cornwall's longest and finest beaches. It is famed for surfing and ideal for families, being lifeguarded.

3 Ballowall Barrow

This remarkable funerary cairn is a complex of barrows and cists from different periods in both the Neolithic and Bronze Ages, the only one of its kind in Cornwall. Long hidden under mining debris until discovered in 1878, Ballowall Barrow faces the setting sun, adding strongly to its womb-shaped symbolism. SW 355 312.

4 Cape Cornwall

Cape Cornwall is a superb viewpoint and an excellent place to watch for dolphins, seals and basking sharks and was long considered Cornwall's most westerly point. Its distinctive chimney was built in 1864 and retained as a navigational mark after the mine beneath was closed. SW 354 318, TR19 7NN

5 Crowns Engine Houses

The coast between Botallack and Pendeen was intensively mined until well into the 20th century. Park by the former Count House at Botallack Mine, SW365333, TR19 7QQ – but please remember that industrial sites can be hazardous and take due care. The Crowns served Boscawen mineshaft. This descended beneath the sea and 1/2 mile from shore to a depth of 1500 ft (455 m). Miners could hear the sea booming overhead.

6 Levant Mine, Trewellard

The Levant complex incudes many chimneys and ruined mine buildings to explore from the Coast Path and adjoining tracks. The mine itself is also open to the public (National Trust, admission fee). Its 1840 engine built by Harvey's of Hayle is the only steam-driven Cornish beam engine operating on its original site.
SW368346, TR19 7SX

7 Gurnard's Head

Gurnard's Head is a 1 km walk from Treen. A splendid viewpoint, it is the site of an Iron Age promontory fort. SW436376, TR26 3DE, please park carefully.

8 St Ives harbour

Artists and writers have long been attracted to St Ives by its natural beauty, especially the clarity of its light and changing skies. It's a delight to explore on foot, especially the harbour and pier.

9 Chûn Castle

This Iron Age hill fort was defended by two concentric stone ramparts standing to a height of 3m plus a pair of rock-cut ditches beyond. It was re-used during the post-Roman period, when it was a centre for the tin trade.

10 Chûn Quoit

One of the best preserved Neolithic megaliths in West Penwith's rich prehistoric landscape, it dates from about 2400 BC. It was probably covered by earth, forming a round barrow (burial site). Location: 1.5 km east of parking on Woon Gumpus Common, SW 394335.

11 Mên-an-Tol

This is a fascinating enigma. Late Neolithic or early Bronze Age, it may once have been part of a stone circle and its holed stone part of a tomb. Some assert that the holed stone is a window on other worlds, others aver it is a source of miraculous healing for rickets, back and limb complaints. It is claimed a woman can conceive by passing through it backwards seven times at full moon, though conventional methods of conception remain popular. SW 426349 on minor road between Morvah and Madron.

12 Lanyon Quoit

Like Chun Quoit, Lanyon Quoit is Neolithic. Wrecked in a storm in 1815, it was rebuilt, but much altered, losing one upright and now standing shorter than before. Park at SW 429337.

13 Carn Euny

Carn Euny (English Heritage, free entry) is a remarkably preserved Romano-British village with courtyard houses joined by thick interlinking walls. Abandoned in the 4th century AD, it overlies a 5th century BC Iron Age village and its long underground stone chamber or 'fogou'. This might have been a cold cellar, or it may have had a ritual or religious purpose. Location SW402288, TR20 8RB, 2 km west of Sancreed. Park at Brane and follow the path for 600 m.

14 Boscawen-ûn

This Bronze Age stone circle comprises nineteen upright stones and a maximum diameter of 25m. However, the central stone stands much higher than the rest. Possibly this stone represents the male phallus, in contrast to the feminine power of the circle. Be that as it may, Boscawen-ûn certainly had great symbolic meaning for its builders, though what that was remains a mystery. SW412274.

15 Trencrom Hill

Enjoy superb views over the Hayle Estuary and St Ives Bay from Trencrom Hill. A walled Neolithic tor enclosure, it was re-used as a hillfort in the Iron Age. From the small car park at Gonew Viscoe (SW518360, TR27 6NH), take the St Michael's Way footpath, then branch left and uphill.

16 Porthgwarra

Among several lovely coves to explore, Porthgwarra is one of the best, though one of the least visited. The Coast Path leads westward by wave-sculpted granite cliffs, which are particularly beautiful in the evening light. In August and early September these cliffs are ablaze with yellow gorse and purple heather. Look out for raptors such as kestrels and buzzards, seabirds including gulls and cormorants, as well as seals, dolphins and basking sharks. TR19 6JR

17 Porthcurno

The large, sandy, lifeguarded beach faces south and is well sheltered by dramatic cliffs, ideal for families and with a car park and café. Nearby is the Porthcurno Telegraph Museum (admission charge) which tells the story of how Porthcurno became the hub of international communications.

18 Treryn Dinas

Treryn Dinas is an impressive headland, twenty minutes' walk from Treen car park (SW394229, TR19 6LQ). Surrounding it are the 2m high ramparts of an Iron Age promontory fort, with a causewayed entrance. Treryn Dinas was reputedly the rendezvous for witches, who cast horrible spells to wreck ships on the rocks below. Balanced on the summit is the famous logan, a 65 ton boulder that could be rocked by hand – until sailors dislodged it in 1824.

19 Penberth Cove

Following the Coast Path east from Treryn Dinas for 1km leads to Penberth Cove, with its granite cottages and fishing boats. Until replaced by an electric winch, the boasts were hauled up here by the 19th century capstan, powered by eight men. TR19 6HJ

20 Lamorna

Lamorna's picturesque cove is approached down a lush, sheltered valley strewn with granite boulders from the old quarries along its sides. The pebble beach is sheltered by a pier, making a small harbour. The Lamorna Wink inn has a great collection of maritime memorabilia and photographs. (A 'kiddlywink' was an unlicensed beer-house.)

21 Mousehole

Winding narrow streets of granite cottages lead down to the harbour, dotted with galleries, pubs, souvenir shops and restaurants, all a delight to explore. From medieval times, Mousehole built its fortunes on fishing, above all on pilchards. Since their sudden decline in the late 19th century, the village has relied chiefly on visitors.

22 Newlyn Harbour

Newlyn's busy harbour is full of interest, especially early in the morning when the lively fish market is open for business. It supports nearly 150 boats of all types, from beam trawlers to long liners, crabbers and small open boats.

23 Penzance, Chapel Street

Chapel Street has some of Penzance's most unusual and historic buildings. Maria Branwell, the mother of novelists Charlotte, Emily and Anne Brontë, lived at number 25, Branwell House. The Egyptian House, built in 1835, combines a flamboyant mix of Egyptian symbols, including lotus columns and Amon sundisks, with a royal Coat of Arms. TR18 4AE

24 The Admiral Benbow

Chapel Street also includes this remarkable 18th century inn packed with fascinating maritime artefacts. These include ships' figureheads, carvings and timbers, model ships, lanterns, ropes, a diver's helmet, a mariner's telescope and much, much more besides. The inn was reputedly headquarters of a smuggling gang called the Benbow Brandy Men and sports the figure of a smuggler on its roof.

25 Jubilee Pool, Penzance

Penzance began to attract tourists in the 19th century, and numbers increased once the railway arrived. The art deco Jubilee Pool at the sea end of Chapel Street was built in 1935 and refurbished in 2021; the pool is the first in Europe to be heated by geothermal energy.

26 Mounts Bay

All around the Bay, from Mousehole to Perranuthnoe, the view is dominated by St Michael's Mount, which can be accessed by a causeway from Marazion at low tide.

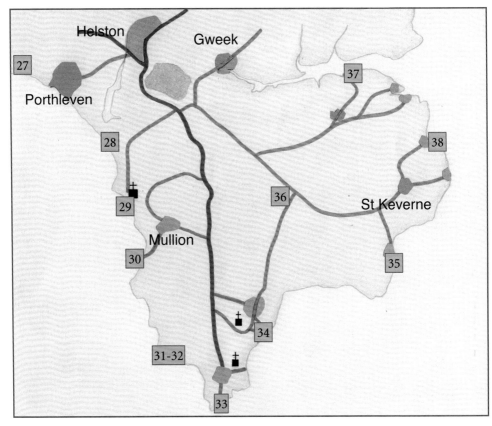

The approximate locations of places on the Lizard Peninsula

27 Wheal Prosper

There is a fine view of Mount's Bay and Wheal Prosper's engine house from Rinsey's National Trust car park (SW 592272, TR13 9TS). A short walk gives a closer view. Sadly, the mine did not prosper: opened in 1860, it closed in 1866, but found a new life in BBC's *Poldark*. Walk 1 km east along the Coastpath to see the spectacular remains of Wheal Trewavas (1834).

28 Loe Bar

Loe Bar is a shingle bank which separates Loe Pool from the sea. It is a site of scientific interest. Because of strong currents, it is a very dangerous place for bathing. The memorial is for the wreck of HMS *Anson* in 1807, with the loss of around 100 sailors. One witness was Henry Trengrouse; he devoted the rest of his life, and much of his money, to developing a 'Rocket Lifesaving Apparatus' – which then saved thousands of other lives.

29 Gunwalloe Church Cove

This pretty cove with its lovely beach is very popular with families, and life-guarded in the high season. There are toilets and a refreshment kiosk. The tiny church is dedicated to St Winwaloe (*c* 460-532) who founded an abbey in Brittany. His parents were part of the major migration in the fifth century AD from Dumnonia (Cornwall and Devon) to Brittany. Just to the north of Church Cove is Dollar Cove, also known as Jangye Ryn. (A shipwreck in the 16th century was the source of the 'dollars'.) It is rockier than Church Cove, and dog-friendly. TR12 7QE

30 Mullion Cove

This picturesque small harbour was built in the 1890s to provide some protection for the small local fishing fleet from the westerly gales which can be very destructive – and are now getting worse through climate change. TR12 7ET

31 Kynance Cove

This is arguably the most dramatic cove on the Cornish coast, with its extraordinary rock stacks and caves, and the contrast between its white sand and the varied colours of the serpentine rocks. Access is by a steep path, and the car park gets full very quickly in summer. SW 687133, TR12 7PJ

32 Serpentine

The Lizard has a strange geological history of continental drift. About 300 million years ago it was part of a 'super-continent' of South America and Africa which briefly collided with Europe, and the Lizard was chipped off and stuck to Cornwall. In Britain, serpentine is unique to the Lizard, and is still quarried and crafted locally. TR12 7PJ

33 Lizard Point

There is a lovely walk to be taken around the Lizard Point from Lizard town. This view is across Housel Bay to the lighthouse.

34 Cadgwith

This is still an active fishing cove, with full-time fishermen working from the beach, rather than a harbour, but now this most photo-genic of villages largely depends on tourism, with holiday lets, an attractive pub and a café. A walk south from the village takes you to the Devil's Frying Pan – a hole in the cliffs where a huge cave col-lapsed. In rough weather, the sea 'boils' in the bottom of the pan. TR12 7JY

35 Coverack

The harbour still holds a number of small fishing craft, but as with Cadgwith tourism is now very important. TR12 6TE

36 Goonhilly Earth Station

This ia a radio-communication site, opened in 1962 to communicate with the satellite Telstar, which enabled live transatlantic television broadcasts, and the broadcast of the Apollo 11 moon landing. The giant dishes, the largest of them 32 m across, are visible from a distance. The original owners BT sold the site in 2014 to another company which uses it for a number of hi-tech purposes. TR12 6LQ

37 Helford

This village is one of the most isolated in Cornwall, and very popular as a second home for celebrities. There is a fine pub overlooking the creek. At one time it was actually a port, where ships loaded ore from barges which brought it from Helston: a Customs house attempted to control the inward flow of smuggled goods. (The location for Daphne du Maurier's novel *Frenchman's Creek* is just a short walk away.) There is a pedestrian ferry across the river to Helford Passage.

38 Porthallow beach

The beach here is entirely pebbles, which, along with its isolation, has kept the village quieter than many Cornish fishing villages – and all the more charming. TR12 6PN

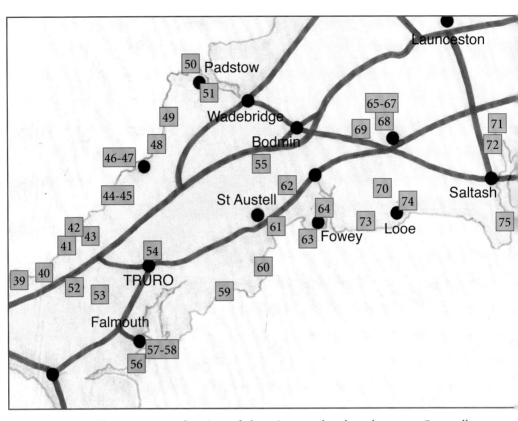

The approximate locations of places in central and south-eastern Cornwall

39 Godrevy

Godrevy's 26 m tall lighthouse marks the Stones Reef, where many ships came to grief before the lighthouse was built in 1859. Author Virginia Woolf spent many summer holidays in St Ives, from where she had a wonderful view to the lighthouse, which later inspired her novel *To the Lighthouse* (1927) – though she set the story in the Hebrides. Location: 1 km north of Gwithian on the B3301. Two National Trust car parks. TR27 5ED

40 Reskajeage Downs

Fine views from the coast path, which here is easy walking – quite level for 5 km. SW 625432.

41 Chapel Porth

Best enjoyed at low tide (and submerged at high tide!) this is a dramatic sandy cove, lifeguarded, popular with families and good for belly-boarding. Towanroath engine house and Wheal Coates stand on the cliffs above. National Trust café, toilets and parking.
SW 695495, TR5 0NS

42 Wheal Coates

The present mine opened in 1802, but records show mining began here in 1692. Three engine houses remain, including iconic Towan-roath (1872), which stands proudly on the cliff edge and pumped water from a 200 m deep shaft, allowing men to mine tin beneath the sea.
SW 703500, TR5 0NU

43 St Agnes Beacon

Enjoy panoramic views from St Agnes Beacon (189 m), the legend-ary home of Bolster, a giant so huge he could stand with one foot on St Agnes Beacon and the other on Carn Brea, nearly ten miles distant. An unashamed chauvinist, he made his wife clear the neighbouring fields of stones. Her apronfulls are seen today as ancient barrows (burial mounds) on the Beacon. Parking is as for Wheal Coates, SW 703500, TR5 0NU. Follow the lane north for 600 m, then the footpath to the summit.

15

44 Perran Sands

Follow the coast path north from Perranporth to enjoy a magnificent view of Perran Sands. Famed for surfing, this 4 km long beach of golden sands is popular with families. Perran Sands is lifeguarded in season and dog friendly.

45 Perran Round

This is a well preserved *plen-an-gwary* or mediaeval amphitheatre for performing plays, though it may well have originally been an Iron Age construction. Park in the hamlet of Rose and follow the signed byway to SW779545, TR4 9PF.

46 Newquay Harbour

Commercial fishing remains important, as the fishing boats in Newquay's harbour prove. Sport fishing is popular too and several Newquay boats offer this, as is well-known to seals which frequent the harbour to beg fish. Dolphins are sometimes seen in the harbour and on boat trips.

47 Newquay Huer's Hut

Between Towan Head and the harbour stands the Huer's Hut. Huers scanned the sea for shoals, especially the once abundant pilchard, alerting fishermen by crying Hevva! Hevva! through long trumpets. The pubs emptied and dinner was left untasted as every able bodied person rushed to man the boats. Once at sea, the fishermen looked to the huer to direct them with his semaphore-like signals.

16

48 Trevelgue Head, Newquay

Trevelgue Head is the site of an Iron Age promontory fort and two early Bronze Age round barrows. It was fortified with extensive ramparts, which are still impressive.

49 Bedruthan Steps

Bedruthan Steps are impressive from every angle and just a ten minute walk from Carnewas car park and its tearooms (SW 850690, PL27 7UW). Legend has it that a giant, Bedruthan, used these sea stacks to make a short cut across the bay. Alas, this far-fetched story appears to be a Victorian invention to attract tourists, and was first recorded in the *West Briton* in 1847.

50 Trevose Head

On a clear day the views from Trevose Head extend 55 km south-west to Pendeen Watch and 65 km north-east to Hartland Point. When Trevose lighthouse was first built in 1847 it was the only light guiding sailors between Land's End and Lundy. Its 27m tall tower has a range of 20 nautical miles. Parking nearby, SW 852762 , PL28 8SH

51 Padstow Harbour

An attractive medley of pubs, shops, restaurants and cafés surround Padstow harbour, where leisure craft mix with fishing boats. Many of the buildings are historic, including the Shipwright's Arms, built in the 18th century as warehousing, possibly a shipbuilder's yard. A short walk leads to St Petroc's, a 15th century church.

52 East Pool

East Pool Mine has two preserved steam engines on separate sites, both owned by the National Trust. Mitchell's Shaft (photo) houses a winding engine built by Holman's of Camborne in 1887. Taylor's Shaft has an 1892 Harvey's engine. Its massive 90 inch engine has a 52 ton bob and a correspondingly solid engine house to support it.

53 Heartlands

This Cornish mining world heritage site, with free entry, gives a comprehensive introduction to Cornwall's mining history. It also offers guided tours of Robinson's Engine House with its preserved 1854 Cornish pumping engine, a film and an excellent museum.

54 Gwennap Pit

This was the site of the largest ever congregation for a John Wesley sermon, estimated (optimistically?) to have been 32,000. The depression was probably created by the surface collapsing into mine workings. SW741400, TR16 5HH

55 Roche Rock

This dramatic outcrop of quartz shorl (tourmalinised granite) stands 20m above the mid-Cornish plateau, with panoramic views to Bodmin Moor and over Cornwall's clay country. Perched on top of Roche Rock is ruined St Michael's chapel, dedicated in 1409, with a lower room for a chaplain or hermit, and the chapel above. SW991596.

18

56 The Pandora Inn

This historic inn at Restronguet Passage was at the site of a ferry crossing. SW815372, TR11 5ST. If you enjoy looking at boats, nearby Mylor Yacht Harbour is well worth a visit.

57 The port of Falmouth

The Fal estuary (Carrick Roads) is a huge natural harbour, and originally its main town was Penryn. Pendennis Castle, seen here from near St Mawes, was built by Henry VIII to protect the estuary, and the town of Falmouth began to develop soon after. From 1689 to 1851 Falmouth 'packet boats' carried mail to all parts of the Empire. In wartime, squadrons of the Navy were stationed here. Falmouth's docks remain a significant part of the town's economy. The excellent National Maritime Museum Cornwall (entry fee) is located here.

58 St Mawes

This attractive former fishing village can be visited by ferry from Falmouth. It too has a castle built by Henry VIII.

59 Portloe

This unspoilt village on the Roseland peninsula still has two full-time fishing boats – but in 1900 it had fifty. Its remoteness and coastal scenery, with fine walks, attract visitors looking for somewhere quiet. Parking at SW938396, TR2 5RA.

60 Mevagissey

Cornwall's second largest fishing harbour, Newlyn being the biggest; it is famous for its network of very narrow streets, these days devoted to shops and eateries for visitors. The name comes from two saints, *Meva hag Ysi*, *hag* being Cornish for 'and'.
Parking at PL26 6SB.

61 Charlestown

This was a fishing village named West Polmear until the 1790s, when its owner Charles Rashleigh developed it as a port to export copper ore and later china clay. The harbour is home to a number of historic sailing ships, and has featured in several TV dramas including *Poldark*.

62 Treffry Viaduct

This impressive structure was built by Joseph Teffry in 1844 across the attractive Luxulyan Valley to carry a horse-drawn railway and also a leat. Treffry had created a new harbour at Par, and the railway connected this with copper mines and quarries to the north. SX 055572

63 Gribbin Head

This is one of the finest viewpoints on the Cornish coast, capped with a 25m tall daymark, built in 1832 to guide ships safely into Fowey Harbour. Gribbin is a haven for many wildflowers and a splendid place to watch birds. Parking at Combe Farm (SX 110512), 2km east along Coastpath.

64 Fowey

With its fine natural harbour, Fowey is a delightful town to explore on foot. Its winding streets are lined with a medley of historic buildings, shops, studios and galleries. Near the delightful Albert Quay is the medieval church, St Fimbarrus, with its magnificent carved ceiling of shields and angels.

Medieval Fowey was one of England's busiest ports, sheltering naval vessels, privateers and pirate ships. It was defended with two 14th century blockhouses. These still exist, as does St Catherine's Castle, a 16th century gun fort (top photo, open free of charge) on the Coastpath by the pretty beach at Readymoney Cove.

French forces attacked in 1457, when Elizabeth Treffry won fame defending Place House. Rebuilt in the 16th and remodelled in the 19th century, Place and its grounds are a splendid backdrop to Fowey (bottom photo). They are best viewed – as is Fowey's fine waterfront – from the Polruan ferry or from the Hall Walk, a lovely 6.4 km/4 mile woodland path rich in wildflowers which links the Polruan and Bodinnick ferries to Fowey.

The Hall Walk diverts to St Wyllow, Lanteglos, a medieval church where novelist Daphne du Maurier of Menabilly near Fowey was married in 1932. It also passes a large granite memorial to Sir Arthur Quiller-Couch, novelist and man of letters, who lived in Fowey.

65 The Cheesewring, Minions

The Cheesewring, a 6m tall granite pile sculpted by wind and weather and so called because it resembles a cider press's 'cheese', stands atop Stowe's Hill, 1.3km north of Minions. Surrounding the summit of Stowe's Hill is an early Neolithic (c 4000-3500 BC) stone enclosure.

66 Minions engine houses

The Minions Heritage Centre has fascinating local historical and geological finds and displays. It is located in the restored Houseman's Engine House, built in the mid-19th century, a time when 4000 miners toiled around Caradon and Minions. Location: 200m east of the Hurlers. The photo shows the Prince of Wales engine house.

67 The Hurlers, Minions

The Hurlers are three Bronze Age stone circles. Legend has it that the Hurlers were men petrified as punishment for playing at hurling on the Sabbath, whilst the nearby standing stones called the Pipers were men similarly punished for impiously playing tunes on a Sunday. Location: 300m north of parking at Minions, SX260712, PL14 5LE.

68 Trethevy Quoit

This impressive Neolithic (c 3700-3500 BC) tomb is 2.7m high and consists of five standing stones and a cover slab. It would originally have been covered by an earth mound. The rear wall has partially collapsed. SX260688, PL14 5JY.

69 Golitha Falls

Follow the banks of the young and fast flowing river Fowey for 750m to the spectacular falls – best seen after rain, though the path may be muddier then! Golitha is ancient woodland, its trees festooned with mosses and lichens. Spring wild-flowers also thrive in the clean, moist air of the valley gorge and many species of woodland birds can be seen. Parking at Draynes Bridge, SX227689, PL14 5ED.

70 Duloe stone circle

This surprisingly impressive stone circle has the smallest diameter of any in Cornwall, consisting of four massive and four smaller stones – and they are of bright white quartz. SX235582, PL14 4PW.

71 Calstock Viaduct

Calstock Viaduct was completed in 1907 with 12,000 concrete blocks, but made to look like stone. Its twelve arches of 18m span still carry the Tamar Valley Line from Plymouth to Gunnislake 39m above the water.

72 Cotehele Quay

Cotehele Quay has a medley of historic buildings, including lime kilns. The Discovery Centre (free entry) tells the story of *Shamrock*, the ketch-rigged Tamar vessel of 1899 moored at the Quay. The centre also has model boats, ships and tableaux explaining how the quay, its boatyard and limekilns looked in their heyday and how salmon were netted on the Tamar.

73 Polperro

Polperro's narrow streets wend down to its harbour, where a pleasing mix of fishing boats and leisure craft provide ever changing interest and movement. It is well known for its charm and the natural beauty of its situation. Polperro is at its best early in the morning and during the winter when fewer visitors come.

74 Looe Harbour

A stroll along East Looe's quay leads past cafés, pubs and shops selling the day's catch to the beach and Banjo Pier. Cross the river by the handsome Victorian bridge and follow the quayside path past the historic Jolly Sailor Inn to meet the bronze statue of Nelson, a one eyed bull Grey Seal, who made Looe Island his home and was a familiar sight around the harbour.

75 Royal Albert Bridge, Saltash

Completed in 1859 after six arduous years, Brunel's 667 m long Royal Albert Bridge was one of his greatest and most enduring triumphs. It still carries mainline trains (far heavier than those of 1859) over the Tamar – a tribute both to Brunel's skill in using bold and experimental technology and to his wise choice of corrosion-resistant wrought iron. The 1961 road bridge stands next to it.

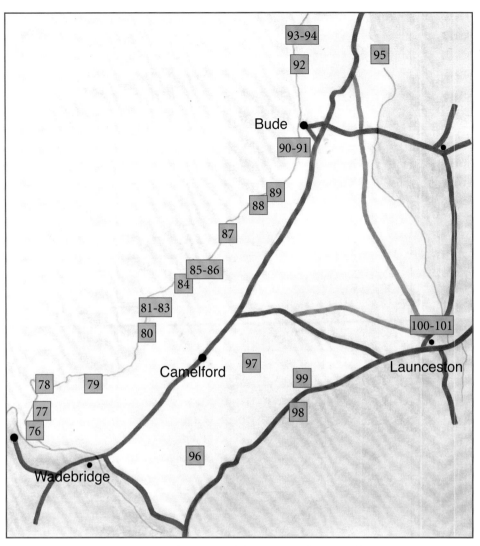

The approximate locations of places in North Cornwall

76 Rock, the ferry to Padstow

The village of Rock is an upmarket holiday location, with a string of boutiques and classy restaurants, but from its car park you have access to the dunes of the estuary, and the pedestrian ferry is also the ideal scenic way to arrive in Padstow. PL27 6FD

77 St Enodoc's Church, Trebetherick

St Enodoc's medieval church, stands just above the surrounding dunes. For three centuries, St Enodoc's was buried in wind-blown sand and was not fully unearthed and the dunes stabilised until 1864. Former Poet Laureate John Betjeman (1906-84) is buried in the churchyard. Betjeman loved this part of Cornwall, celebrating it in many poems. Location, 700 m south of Daymer Bay car park, SX 927777, PL27 6SA

78 Polzeath Beach

Polzeath's large, sandy beach is popular with both families and surfers, from beginners to experts. It is well served with cafes and pubs and has a handy car park SX 937789, PL27 6TB.

79 Port Isaac

Sheltering in a rocky cove on the north Cornish coast, Port Isaac is a fishing village of real charm. Its beautiful situation and narrow streets of 18th and 19th century houses built in local stone and slate have made it an ideal backdrop for films such as *Saving Grace* and *Fisherman's Friends* (the singers were and still are based here) to TV dramas from *Poldark* to the long running series *Doc Martin*. Park at PL29 3SG.

Sept 2022

80 Trebarwith Strand

The Port William Inn looks out over Trebarwith Strand. The inn's fine collection of local photographs show sailing ships, lifeboats and fishing scenes and the now vanished industry of collecting sand from Trebarwith Strand, a low tech activity using shovels and donkeys.

81 Cliffs south of Tintagel

The dramatic Coastpath north from Trebarwith Strand passes several disused slate quarries, worked from the 15th to the early 20th centuries. Look down (carefully!) from the cliff tops to see the ruins of slate-splitting sheds, tramways, mine buildings and the impressive 24 m tall pinnacle of inferior slate left standing in the midst of Lanterdan Quarry.

82 Tintagel Island

The promontory and island may have been one of many on the Cornish coast occupied during the Iron Age. Certainly, the site was intensively occupied during the 5th to 7th centuries. The castle (English Heritage, entrance fee) was developed in the 13th century and became widely known through the legends of King Arthur.

83 Tintagel village

The oldest building is the Old Post Office (National Trust, entry fee). Originally built in the 14th century to the plan of a manor house, it has served many purposes, the last as a letter receiving office in the 1870s.

84 Rocky Valley, Bossiney

Deeply wooded Rocky Valley runs by a series of waterfalls in a 20m deep canyon to meet the sea. Rocky Valley is famed for its mysterious rock carvings. Some assert they are Early Bronze Age, others favour the Iron Age. A more recent school of thought suggests the patterns were carved within the last 250 years by the miller of Trevillet Mill or his apprentices. Park at SX073891.

85 Boscastle Harbour

This is the only viable harbour on a long stretch of Cornwall's rocky north coast, well sheltered by high cliffs, plus two stone walls built in 1584 by Sir Richard Grenville. Boscastle was a bustling commercial port before the railway reached North Cornwall in 1893.

86 Boscastle from above

It is well worth climbing the coast path to either side for magnificent views over the harbour entrance. The western cliff, Willapark, also gives a view of the Forrabury stitches, a medieval strip farming survival.

87 Crackington Haven

Deep combes, streams and water-falls give Crackington a special, stark beauty. Equally striking are its folded, twisted rocks. Known to geologists as the 'Crackington Formation', they are sheets of inter-bedded Carboniferous sandstone and shale. These extraordinary rocks are best seen on Cambeak, 1.8km west along the Coastpath.

88 Millook

The dramatic rock formations at Millook, chevron folds of interbedded sandstones and shales, are part of the 'Crackington Formation'. Dating from the Carboniferous period (*c*345-280 million years ago), they testify to enormous tectonic forces at play during this mountain building episode. SX185000, EX23 0DQ

89 Widemouth Bay

Widemouth is a huge lifeguarded beach of golden sand, with convenient parking and a café. It is ideal for surfing, from beginner to advanced level and home to surf schools. Widemouth is also popular with families. At low tide there are hundreds of rock pools to explore. EX23 0AW

90 Bude, looking North

One of North Cornwall's finest views looks out over Bude Haven and Summerleaze beach from the former Coastguard lookout on Compass Point. Known as the 'Pepper Pot', it was built of local sandstone in 1835 and modelled on the Temple of Winds in Athens, with the points of the compass inscribed on each face.

91 Bude Castle

This was built by the inventor Sir Goldsworthy Gurney around 1830, the first building ever to be constructed on a concrete raft 'floating' on the sand dunes. It is now home to an excellent local museum (free admission). EX23 8LG

92 GCHQ

These extraordinary dishes are visible from miles away along the coast. This is a Government eaves-dropping centre. NB Trespassing here is a specific criminal offence!

93 Higher Sharpnose Point, Morwenstow

'A stretch of bold and rocky shore, an interchange of lofty headland and deep and sudden gorge, the valleys gushing with torrents which bound rejoicingly to the sea,' enthused Parson Hawker, describing his clifftop rambles (sometimes coloured by opium). Follow Hawker's footsteps along the coast-path for 1.3 km south-west from Morwenstow to Higher Sharpnose Point for superb views.

94 Morwenstow Church and Vicarage

Morwenstow's exceptional church is noted for its Norman arches with their zigzag patterns, original waggon roofs,medieval carved bench ends and a rood screen. The church was restored by its parson poet, Robert Stephen Hawker.

95 Tamar Lake Walk

A broad, well surfaced and mainly level path, suitable for pushchairs, wheelchairs and bikes, surrounds the beautiful Upper Tamar Lake. Take binoculars – it is a great place to watch a variety of waterfowl and woodland birds too. Allow at least 1 3/4 hours for the full circuit of the lake, 5.2 km. EX23 9SB

96 Blisland

Blisland is one of Bodmin Moor's most attractive villages. The Blisland Inn, with its collections of local photographs and toby jugs, stands on one side of the large village green and its church, described by Sir John Betjeman as 'dazzling and amazing', on the other. Most impressive are the barrel-vaulted ceilings with their carved bosses and angels. Other notable features include the carved Norman font, 17th century pulpit and 1604 Royal Coat of Arms. PL30 4JF

97 Rough Tor

This and its neighbour Brown Willy are Cornwall's highest points. From the car park at SX138819, a walk to the right around the hill will take you through a Bronze Age settlement, with hut circles, to the Fernacre stone circle (SX145800).

98 Jamaica Inn

The building dates from 1750, and was a staging post on the main road across Bodmin Moor, then a temperance hotel. It was made famous by Daphne du Maurier's novel, and is much visited today.

99 Altarnun

One of Cornwall's prettiest villages, Altarnun derives its name from its church's dedication to the mother of St David, and means 'Altar of St Nonn'. It is noted for its 33m tall tower, Norman font, Celtic cross and wonderfully carved bench ends. Opposite St Nonna's is a 15th century packhorse bridge.

100 Launceston

Launceston has a long and fascinating history. Perched on a hilltop 2 km west of the Tamar, it was ideally placed to control traffic on the main road into Cornwall. The town has three parts, the Norman castle town, an earlier settlement of Saxon origin (St Stephens or *Lanstefan*) across the valley, and Newport in between. Every type of building since the Norman Conquest is represented in Launceston. Lawrence House with its excellent museum, Southgate, the Church of St Mary Magdalene and the castle bailey are outstanding.

101 Launceston Southgate

Of Launceston's three medieval town gates, only Southgate remains.

Some other Bossiney books about Cornwall

About St Michael's Mount
About Tintagel
Cornish Engine Houses
Cornwall Beach and Cove Guide – North Coast
Discover North Cornwall
The Lizard Peninsula
Penzance to Land's End

Shortish Walks near Land's End
Really Short Walks – West Cornwall
Shortish Walks on and near the Lizard
Really Short Walks – St Ives to Padstow
Shortish Walks – Bodmin Moor
Really Short Walks – North Cornwall
Shortish Walks – North Cornwall
Writers' Walks on the Cornish Coast